The ABC's of Incivility at Work

A Cautionary Tale
of Draggles and Wowzers

Céleste Grimard

Copyright © 2019
Céleste Grimard, Canada
All rights reserved. All materials on these pages are copyrighted by Céleste Grimard. Reproduction, modification, storage of all or a part of this book in a retrieval system or retransmission, in any form or by any means, electronic, mechanical or otherwise is strictly prohibited without prior written permission from the author.
ISBN-13: 978-1720526940
Imprint by KDP

This book is fictional in nature. Any resemblance to individuals or events is coincidental.
Céleste Grimard illustrated this book.

ACKNOWLEDGMENTS

I thank Jerôme Gagnon, Michel Cossette, and Miguel Olivas-Luján for their helpful comments on earlier drafts of this book. I also thank countless workers who have shared with me their stories about life at work.

ONCE UPON A TIME, not so long ago and not too far away, Draggles from Planet Draggle learned that life existed beyond their moons and suns. Wowzers from Planet Wowzie, a nearby planet in the same galaxy as Planet Draggle, had beamed down to Planet Draggle from their 11,111 space flying machines and surprised a motley crew of young Draggles learning about leadership in Classroom. What happened next is a long story filled with encounters, protocol, and pizza as Wowzers and Draggles became acquainted with each other.

Wowzer Yolanda, whose specialty was courtesy, was in charge of the mission to Planet Draggle. She loved to meet other species, and, with her many eyes could easily see that Planet Draggle's oceans were teaming with high-grade Zolto crystals.

Zolto crystals were essential to Wowzer survival. Wowzers spontaneously lost their eyesight during jon marr, their coming of age ritual. They had been using synthetic Zolto crystals to recuperate their vision. Unfortunately, synthetic Zolto crystals were of poor quality and in limited supply. Moreover, their sole manufacturer (from another planet) took advantage of their monopoly by upping the price of Zolto crystals on a whim.

Planet Draggle's leader was X-Pert Xavier, who considered himself to be an expert on everything, even things that he knew nothing about. One fine day, when Wowzer Yolanda inquired about the exquisite, shining triangular crystal on Draggle uniforms, Draggle

Xavier explained that the crystal was cool to look at and

handy for slicing pizza, their favorite food, but had absolutely no other use. "It's a piece of cheap cr--."

This was the moment that Wowzer Yolanda was waiting for since they had first made contact with Draggles. Wowzer Yolanda asked Draggle Xavier if Wowzers could acquire a large quantity of these crystals over the next millennia. In exchange, Wowzers would offer Draggles their state-of-the-art pizza slicing technology. Of course, Draggle Xavier accepted immediately.

After Wowzer Yolanda negotiated a favorable deal for Zolto crystals with Draggle Xavier, Wowzers worked with Draggles to establish a process for scooping, compressing, and packing large quantities of Zolto crystals in zip balls which were robotically transported on the new space elevator to Planet Wowzie. Within a month, the process seemed to be working fine. So, Wowzers entrusted Zolto Plant to Draggles and announced that they would go home to Planet Wowzie, returning to Planet Draggle only once in two green moons to maintain the technology.

In the absence of Wowzers, Draggles populated Zolto Plant with the best graduates of Classroom to oversee the Zolto crystal mining-transporting-deal maintenance process: the Draggle UltraOffice Dwellers (DUDs). Draggle Xavier was in charge.

Even though the process worked fine when managed by Wowzers, as time passed, production levels began to decline to a dribble. Communications from Zolto Plant to Wowzers became sporadic, confusing, and unpleasant. Something wasn't working. Soon enough, two green moons appeared above Planet Draggle.

This was the signal that Wowzers needed to return to Planet Draggle and investigate what caused the drop in production and the patchy communications. While a crew performed the necessary maintenance on the Zolto crystal mining technology, a small team of highly perceptive Wowzers observed and encountered Draggle DUDs at Zolto Plant. After a reasonable period of observation and interaction, these Wowzers returned to Planet Wowzie and reported that they had observed the following characters at Zolto Plant.

ALL ABOUT ME AGNES doesn't mind drawing attention to herself. In fact, she constantly brags about herself, her family, her accomplishments, her … everything! She hogs talk time in meetings, during lunch and coffee breaks, and around the office. She loves to show off about all that is well in her world, but she also likes to overshare about all that is not well. All About Me Agnes spontaneously talks about the results of her gynecological exam, her inability to find the Draggle of her dreams, her fabulous weekend on the Planet O' Suns, and any other personal issues that she happens to have. "Me, myself, and I" is her motto.

All About Me Agnes keeps talking even if she's disturbing her colleagues or disrupting their work. In fact, she doesn't care if she's disturbing or disrupting them because that's not important. What IS important is what's going on in her life right now. And when the attention shifts to someone else, you can hear her sigh out of boredom or irritation or see her play on her phone, texting her friends and posting about herself on social media. In fact, the best way to make her disappear is to shift your attention to someone else.

The ABC's of Uncivil Behavior at Work

Me! Me! Me!
Pay attention to me!

BUSY BOB says that he is juggling lots of balls and is too busy to be given additional work. He feels that he has been overloaded with work, even though he has the same amount of work as everyone else. Busy Bob scolds Draggle Xavier for overloading him. "I can't keep up. I have more work than I can possibly do in a day. That's majorly unfair," he says to Draggle Xavier directly or to coworkers while Draggle Xavier is within antenna-shot.

In fact, the issue isn't Busy Bob's workload; it's his inability to set priorities, organize and focus on his work, and get it done. He neither works harder nor smarter. He's unable to manage a reasonable workload. Busy Bob is so busy complaining about his workload throughout the day that he loses the precious time he needs to actually do his work. In fact, his complaining and inefficiently ways are responsible for his being busy.

He tries to lighten his load by farming out work to his coworkers or by simply letting the ball drop so often that he can no longer be trusted to do the work. He wants others to think he's busy so that they don't give him more work to do. And it's working!

Busy Bob's cousin **DABBLER DELMAR** is also busy, and, like Busy Bob, he doesn't get his work done. Dabbler Delmar is busy doing everything but his job: he's supposed to be packing the crystals, but he's creating videos of crystals. He does what he wants to do regardless of his job responsibilities. He tells others that he has too much work to do and should get an assistant.

I spend so much time complaining that I don't have time to do my work. Poor me!

CREDIT HOGGING CLIFF likes to talk about his successes. He doesn't give credit where it's due. He takes credit for his work – and yours. He asks you for help with his work, but he takes all the credit for it. Credit Hogging Cliff selectively recognizes the accomplishments of some coworkers (those who are his friends), but not others (Draggles he considers to be competitors). When someone mentions an idea to him, he brings it up in a meeting as though it was his own idea.

He loves to be the center of attention, and he takes advantage of situations to make himself look good. In fact, Credit Hogging Cliff hogs attention: he loves to give presentations on team projects, knowing that observers assume that the person presenting the project is the leader and has contributed more than others.

But when things go wrong, Credit Hogging Cliff is nowhere to be seen. Nothing can ever be his fault because he's too successful to fail at anything. He doesn't take responsibility for his own (negative) actions. In fact, he only cares about taking credit for others' actions… and only when they have positive outcomes.

The ABC's of Uncivil Behavior at Work

Our successes are due to my brilliance.
Our team wouldn't be successful without me.

DOWNER DWIGHT casts a shadow over everything that doesn't meet his expectations (and, indeed, nothing is to his liking). The suns never shine on Downer Dwight who is constantly complaining, irritated, annoyed, moody, sensitive, negative, unhappy, blah...

As Downer Dwight drags himself down the hallway, he sighs loudly, and a shadow appears all around him. In fact, you can see the shadows intensifying around him, and his coworkers begin to feel miserable and question Zolto Plant. Draggle Xavier and Zolto Plant become easy fodder for complaints as the work ambiance darkens.

Downer Dwight jumps at Draggle Xavier's and others' inevitable missteps, "If there's something to complain about, I'll complain. And, there's always something to complain about."

The ABC's of Uncivil Behavior at Work

Work sucks! I hate it, and you should too!

EDITH EATER is hungry. She doesn't have a chance to eat before arriving at work, or maybe she does, but she would rather nosh at work – usually at the lunch table but also at her work station. She's gobbling a meal of garlic sausage, fried onions, beans and curry rice and drowning it in strong coffee. There are spills, odors, slurps, spits, farts, burps. Sticky fingers. Teeth flossing. Gargling and rinsing. Spitting into cups. After 20 minutes, Eden Eater crushes the empty food and drink containers, casts them aside towards others or the floor and pulls out…dessert.

Throughout the day, the whole Zolto Plant hears her crunching on carrots and celery, popping corn, or crumpling bags. Eden Eater has no idea that her coworkers are disgusted by the spectacle, the sounds, and the odors. Moreover, her stocks of granola bars and other snacks at her work station attract rodents to Zolto Plant.

The ABC's of Uncivil Behavior at Work

So what if I make a bit of noise or a mess…or if I attract mice to the work area?

FASHION FANNIE is decked out. She has large hoop earrings, a perfect makeup job, crystals embedded in her long gel claws, and long hair that flows around her head one minute and is pulled into a high ponytail the next minute. Fashion Fannie spends her time at work copiously brushing and flipping her hair, sometimes inspecting it for split ends. Her lipstick often needs to be refreshed. She carries her make-up kit in her designer satchel bag, which matches her knee-high boots and her preppy hipster look. Who knows, she might be going to a fashion show or an upscale club after work…or the beach.

At times, she takes the casual dress code one step too far: she wears crop tops, tank tops/halters, cut-offs,

I grace this team with my presence.

sheer clothing, strapless (braless) dresses, flip flops, and visible underwear. Oh my! Fashion Fannie's focus on fashion distracts her and others from their work.

Fashion Fannie thinks she could teach a thing or two about style to **UNKEMPT UMBERTO**. They both groom themselves at work, but Unkempt Umberto picks his nose, clips his nails, sticks his claws into every orifice, and scratches, scratches, scratches. Whereas Fashion Fannie's coworkers choke on her perfume, Unkempt Umberto's coworkers choke on his bad breath and body odor….and flatulence. You can easily tell that he considers deodorant and showers optional.

Unkempt Umberto thinks he's rocking the casual dress code by wearing baggy, wrinkled, torn, and soiled clothing as well as dirty runners or socks with sandals. His bounteous and matted hair protrudes from his chest, nose, and ears. His fingers and teeth are stained yellow from smoking. He can be heard blowing his nose, coughing, hacking, belching, and moaning. He can be seen spitting on the floor or sidewalk or in the garbage can. And yet, he has no idea why his coworkers choke or gag in his presence.

GERMY GEORGE should have stayed home. He's coughing and hacking and groaning in pain, propelling thousands of germ particles and droplets into the air. His coworkers try to avoid him, and they cringe when he accidentally touches their work or them. But, he scoffs at the suggestion that he might pass on his illness to coworkers.

Germy George is wasting his day zombieing his way through work and sitting most of the day in front of a blank screen. He's not getting much work done at all. In fact, he's not getting ANY work done, and he's hindering the work of others as they try to avoid him and anything he touches.

Germy George prides himself on being "reliable" and never missing a single day of work at Zolto Plant… ever. He even chastises coworkers who are thoughtful enough to know when to stay home. Germy George doesn't realize that it would much more considerate and appropriate if he simply stayed home and rested instead of showing up at work just to do nothing useful.

The ABC's of Uncivil Behavior at Work

Who me, sick?

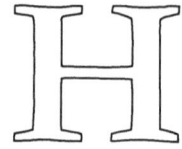

HAROLD HOGGLER & HAROLD HAGGLER, cousins to All About Me Agnes, are twins. Harold Hoggler hogs talk time in work meetings. He's got lots to say, much of which is irrelevant. He drags on and on, and Draggle Xavier can't cut in. Harold Hoggler's specialty is hijacking conversations. He considers his own issues to be "urgent," and he expects others to bow down to them. After all, his priorities and interests are more important than yours, aren't they? And an assembled group of people is the perfect forum for presenting his personal agenda. Harold Hoggler sidetracks meetings by diverting a discussion about someone else to himself and taking over the meeting agenda. Sigh!

His twin, Harold Haggler, considers everything to be negotiable: from work hours to what gets done at Zolto Plant, how work is assigned, pay levels, and anything else under the suns. Absolutely everything is on the bargaining table, and he won't accept "no" for an answer. Midway through the day, when Harold Haggler realizes how much work he has yet to do, he begins several rounds of negotiation with Draggle Xavier to reduce his workload or, at the very least, his personal arrangements to accommodate his unique personal circumstances.

I push till I get my way, then I push some more!

I

ILL-MANNERED AND VERY IMPOLITE IDA never says *please, thank you, excuse me, I'm sorry, I made a mistake,* or anything else remotely resembling politeness. She spews forth vulgarities whenever she's expected to focus on work. Her communications with others are void of courtesies and politeness. She won't lower herself to show respect towards others, particularly Draggle Xavier.

Ill-Mannered and Very Impolite Ida and her cousin **RUDE RANDY** are a tag team combo who feel Entitled to Everything. They are right, and others are wrong. They don't pitch in and help when help is needed. In fact, they slow down work processes by not responding in a reasonable time period to emails and phone calls. Cooperation, teamwork, and facilitating others' work and aren't words in their vocabulary. If you're stuck in a stall without toilet paper and ask them to give you a few sheets, they simply ignore you. They make a game of closing the elevator door when they see you arrive. They don't hold any doors open. In fact, they wait at the door so that others can open it for them.

The ABC's of Uncivil Behavior at Work

You talking to me?
Don't expect me to help out with your problems!
Why say "thank you" when you should be
thanking ME?

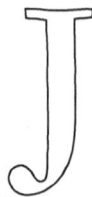

JUDGING JUDITH acts like the judge and jury of all that happens in Zolto Plant. In her mind, her opinion supersedes that of others, and she knows best. Instead of immersing herself in her work and trying to contribute as much as possible, Judging Judith sits back and evaluates, judges and criticizes all that is said and done. Judging Judith doubts her coworkers' judgments regarding their responsibilities. She automatically sees the pimples, problems, and weaknesses in other Draggles' work and the person in charge of it (Draggle Xavier). "I could do a way better job."

SUSPICIOUS SUSAN, second cousin to Judging Judith, distrusts colleagues and goes out of her way to prove that her trust can't be earned. Ever. No one is worthy of her trust. She takes notes about the time you got in, how long you're gone for a break, the time you leave… She carefully compiles facts and data about your whereabouts and makes it her business to inform management about her "findings." Never mind that, while she's busy doing that, she's not working at all …

BASIL BULLY, first cousin to Judging Judy, thinks that others (especially those with less power) are idiots.

"They're all a bunch of stupid jerks." Sarcasm and put-downs are Basil Bully's weapons of choice. Whenever someone is talking, Basil Bully rolls his eyes and sighs, "What idiots!" Basil Bully's special talent is public humiliation and reputation-ruining. If you befriend him (or not), he teases you, makes demeaning, rude, or derogatory remarks, addresses you in unprofessional terms ("Hey Pussy!"), insults you, reveals to others what you shared with him in confidence ("Still have an incontinence problem?"), undermines your credibility in front of others, makes digs or mean-spirited jokes at your expense, and spreads gossip or rumors about you. Even if Basil Bully isn't your boss, he finds a way to publicly reprimand you about "something."

You suck!

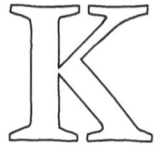

KARLA KERFUFFLE makes a fuss about anything and everything. An unfriendly Draggle, her moodiness, bitchiness, and general contrary nature drag others down. Everything's a hassle, a problem, an issue, and an inconvenience. Karla Kerfuffle is super sensitive, and if anyone looks at her the wrong way, there'll be hell to pay. What was a minor glitch becomes a huge issue involving many Draggles.

Karla Kerfuffle has temper tantrums. She is not only verbally irritable but also physically bad-tempered, on the verge of being intimidating, so much so that coworkers feel that they mustn't talk to her if they want to survive another day. She loves giving dirty looks without provocation. She's unsympathetic to others' situations and would rather turn her back than help out.

She bangs her fists on her desk, swears, rants, throws stuff around the room, and glares at Draggle Xavier when she learns that she needs to re-do some (poorly done) work. "Draggle Xavier is so demanding and rigid. Cut me some slack!" Karla Kerfuffle argues for clemency till she's purple in the face, not realizing that Draggle Xavier may give in now just to get her off his back, but be extra vigilant in evaluating her performance in the next cycles. Karla Kerfuffle may win the battle, but she will lose the war.

I make a big deal out of everything!

LATE AND LEAVING LARRY never arrives to work on time. In fact, he's predictably unpredictable. Moreover, Late and Leaving Larry often leaves work before the end of the official work day. "Work hours don't fit my personal schedule, and I don't want to be here. Who cares if my coworkers need my help? I don't!" He comes and goes when he pleases. When Late and Leaving Larry does show up for work, he's there physically, but not in spirit. He can often be found on his cellphone throughout the workday and during meetings.

Late and Leaving Larry is usually late for meetings, or he simply doesn't show up. He is inattentive and either changes the subject or doesn't participate. He loves to hold side conversations during a meeting or presentation. Even when Draggle Xavier is in the middle of a meeting presentation, Late and Leaving Larry loudly packs up his stuff and walks out. So what if it makes noise and distracts his coworkers! Apparently, he's got things to do and people to see that are so important that he needs to leave … now. What a team player!

His cousin, **ALEX AWOL** is rarely seen in Zolto Plant. Is he working from home or visiting clients? Is he sick? No one really knows for sure, not even his boss. When at work, he avoids interacting with coworkers and participating in team activities. He takes extra-long coffee breaks, checks social media (and, in fact, takes selfies at local coffee shops four times a day), sends messages and chats with friends, and does personal work for his side-business. His long weekends are extra-long due to "unfortunate" illnesses that occur coincidentally on Mondays. He stays away from work when he feels the slightest headache coming on. And he strategically obtains doctors' notes precisely when the workload gets heavy or reports are due. Is Alex AWOL really sick? No one knows for sure, but his coworkers saw him at the pizza parlor when he said he was sick. To top it off, without giving any notice, during busy production seasons, Alex AWOL heads over to Planet O' Suns for a few weeks to recover from the stress of Zolto Plant.

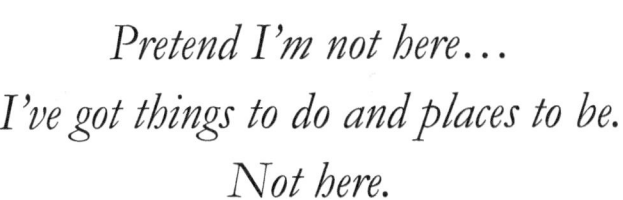

Pretend I'm not here…
I've got things to do and places to be.
Not here.

MOOCHING MILDRED is a sluggish slacker who wants a free ride – good pay for doing the least amount of work possible. She doesn't do her share of the work. In fact, she doesn't do very much work at all. Instead, she relies on others to pick up the slack. Sometimes, she begs Draggle Xavier to reduce her workload, but normally her coworkers just give in and do the work for her (reluctantly). She's the weakest link on a team. An eternal procrastinator, she hopes that the team will just ignore her and do her part of the work. She's gotten away with having her tasks in several team projects done for her by faking serious personal issues at critical times or by massaging the egos of team members ("You're much better at this than I am...").

Mooching Mildred has a reputation for being unreliable and not following through on her commitments. She will promise but not deliver. She might agree to something in private, but deny it in public. Like Alex AWOL, She will often call in sick, leaving coworkers to shoulder a heavy load. She will even lie to avoid work.

Mooching Mildred mooches in every way possible. Even at team potluck lunches, she can be seen taking the "best" for herself (the best seat, the last donut, the biggest slice of pizza, etc.) without contributing anything at all or bringing something 'minor' such as a bag of chips. Eventually, this social loafing, untrustworthiness, and undependability will catch up to her, but she's milking it for as long as she can.

Just do my work for me; it'll be easier and faster for you (and me). And don't count on me to keep my promises.

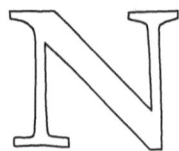

NEEDY NED needs others' constant attention, affirmation, and assistance to do his work. He inconveniences others with his work questions, and he asks too many favors. Needy Ned is insecure, and he doesn't trust that he understands what he should be doing or, indeed, anything correctly. He talks to Draggle Xavier and others before and during work hours, during breaks, and after work. He frequently steps into Draggle Xavier's office to say hello, and he sends lots of written messages, all to make sure that he's on the right page. He needs Draggle Xavier and others to pat him on the back and explain everything to him ... one more time.

Needy Ned's second cousin, **INSECURE IRMA**, projects her own insecurities onto others and has an unhealthy need to compare herself to others. She can't help but measure her own worth against other people's successes. If others succeed, she feels threatened by them, she envies them, and she feels bad about herself. If others fail, she laughs and secretly rejoices. She may even bring others to have doubts about themselves: "That's meaningless," or "Been there, done that."

The ABC's of Uncivil Behavior at Work

*Please help me.
I depend heavily on you to get my work done.*

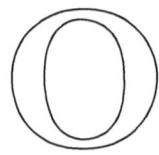

OPINIONATED OLGA could care less that experts say x, y, and z. If her experience differs from what experts say, then her personal view of the world, a sample of one, is what matters. "I already know everything that I need to know; why should I listen to others. I'm right, and everyone else is an idiot. If you don't do things my way, then you've got some screws loose. Don't argue with me; you'll lose. Let me set you straight on things." Opinionated Olga thinks nothing of calling out Draggle Xavier and others on so-called errors, or challenging others on topics that are way off the subject at hand. "Planet Draggle isn't an oblate spheroid; it's round. Perfectly round. I saw it in a cartoon."

The ABC's of Uncivil Behavior at Work

I should be the boss. I know everything.

PERSONAL SPACE PRUNELLA AND PIERRE stand too close to you and violate your personal space. As you step back, they move forward. Personal Space Prunella touches people inappropriately, frequently causing them to recoil. She tries to draw you into a conversation on personal matters despite your discomfort. She touches, fondles, and rearranges your stuff in your workstation. She even goes into your workstation when you're not there and takes your stuff or modifies it without prior agreement. To top it off, she freely reads your emails and forwards your personal (embarrassing) emails to others. Your personal information becomes public.

Since she loves to sit close to people, Personal Space Prunella can be seen cozying up her chair next to yours at a meeting or in the lunchroom. She leans over and looks at what you're reading or working on. She even freely joins you while you're at a coffee shop enjoying what you had hoped was a quiet time to reflect.

Watch out for Personal Space Pierre in the washroom! He enjoys watching the guy at the urinal next to his taking a leak, and he tries to start a conversation with him. He also tries to look into or 'accidentally' go into the ladies' washroom. If you watch where his gaze is directed, you will feel exposed. Is his middle name "Leering" by any chance? Finally, he may be seen spying on people online or in person, "Did you know that there are two Draggles with your last name on the Wanted List?" He will "accidentally" enter your office while you're away or follow you to a coffee shop – just like Personal Space Prunella.

Whatcha doing? Mind if I cozy over?

QUIVERING QUENTIN always finds ways to not take responsibility for himself and his actions. He never owns up to mistakes that he has made, nor does he own up to breaking or damaging things. His will open his eyes wide or point his finger towards someone else as he feigns ignorance about a problem. "Someone broke the printer? Not me!" Given his sensitivity to any critiques, his lower lip quivers at the slightest mention that he may have slipped up.

If it seems that all evidence is pointing in his direction, he finds excuses such as sickness, personal crises, or stress. But, his favorite excuses are unclear directions, system problems, communication mix-ups, work issues, and uncooperative coworkers. You can bet that he'll blame his poor personal performance on factors outside his control and possibly even...you!

Quivering Quentin's cousin, **BY THE BOOK BERTRAM,** takes responsibility but only for a narrowly defined set of tasks. If something needs to be done but it's not in his job description, he looks the other way. He doesn't step out of his comfort zone or look out for the team's needs.

The ABC's of Uncivil Behavior at Work

It's not my fault. It's his fault.

RUDE RANDY, whom we've already met, is someone who simply doesn't realize that he can get further by being polite and that we catch more flies with honey than with vinegar. He is inattentive when Draggle Xavier or others talk to him (sometimes interrupting, sometimes checking messages on his communication device, sometimes rolling his eyes and looking disgusted, sometimes changing the topic, and sometimes even walking away). But, when he has demands, Rude Randy is in your face with his claws waving fiercely. He argues his point till you give up, give in, and silently retreat from the room.

Rude Randy's cousin, **ROUGH RICKY**, is physically aggressive and careless with the objects around him. He can be seen pounding his fists on tables, slamming doors, kicking boxes, or throwing his computer on the floor. He simply doesn't respect company property. He leaves exterior doors unlocked and windows open, and he forgets confidential files at the coffee shop.

The ABC's of Uncivil Behavior at Work

*You might call me aggressive,
but I'm just standing up for myself.
And, if you'd just shut up, you'd hear me better.*

S

SOCIALIZING SALLY rarely focuses on her work. She chats throughout the workday whenever the urge strikes her.

She can be found standing at someone's work station or door while they're trying to work or even when they're on the phone. "I've got lots of important and clever stuff to say to folks, and it can't wait till coffee time." These side conversations distract her coworkers, but they continue even though Draggle Xavier has told Socializing Sally to cease and desist. "So what if it bothers others?"

Aside from holding loud conversations within earshot of Draggles trying to work, she may laugh loudly, unaware that it's disturbing. She may play loud music or even sing, hoping that others will come and talk with her. Needless to say, Socializing Sally has trouble getting her own work done. Somehow, the day flies by, and she has accomplished…nothing.

The ABC's of Uncivil Behavior at Work

*You say that I'm distracting,
but I'm just being friendly.*

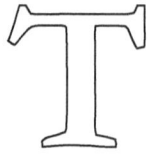

TECHNOLOGY TOMMY loves to use the printer and photocopier for personal purposes such as printing books or taking "bum" pictures. He tends to hog the copier or collective printer and prefers to not clean up after himself in the photocopy room. If there's a problem with the printer or copier, he will leave it in 'error' mode, jammed, with a low toner signal, or without paper. Shards of paper are everywhere.

If that's not bad enough, Technology Tommy is a security risk to Zolto Plant. Ever so trusting and curious, he can be found clicking on spam, popups, and executable attachments sent from unknown parties. Let's just say that he's intimately familiar with worms, Trojans, and spyware. Moreover, when he isn't sending others aggressively worded flaming emails or nasty notes about you, he loves to "spread joy" by copying the entire office on joke emails or trying to sell personal items for "discounted" prices. His copious emails flood and slow down the system.

Technology Tommy is distracted by technology, but so is **TEXTING TIMMY** who is constantly using some kind of electronic device, despite Draggle Xavier's rules that personal communication devices must not be used during work time and, especially, meetings. Texting Timmy enjoys checking written messages, taking selfies, watching movies or sports, listening to music, and doing personal Dragglenet searches during work hours. When Draggle Xavier reminds Texting Timmy to put away his communication device and get to work, he puts it on his lap, and he continues texting. He doesn't realize that Draggle Xavier sees this *lap texting*. Texting Tommy is at work, but not working. When other coworkers see that Texting Tommy is distracted by his devices, they take out their devices too.

I've got urgent texting to do.

U OWE ME UMA steals from Zolto Plant. Oh, she doesn't consider it to be stealing. Nope! She figures that it's part of her total compensation package, a small perk in exchange for her toil. Besides, she does "think" about work while at home, so she should get paid for it – in kind. Right?

U Owe Me Uma brings home pens and staplers, paper and envelopes, toilet paper and chairs, laptops and printers…you name it. In fact, she does her "school supply shopping" for her children at work.

But, there's more. U Owe Me Uma engages in time theft from Zolto Plant. She arrives at work on time, but she spends the first 30 minutes getting ready for work (makeup, coffee, socializing, etc.). Throughout the day, she does personal business and Facebooking at work. She goes out on shopping sprees during business hours, takes extra-long lunch breaks, and goes outside every hour for "smoke breaks" that never last less than 20 minutes at a time…

Sigh! She doesn't know why she doesn't get more work done.

The ABC's of Uncivil Behavior at Work

*What's the big deal if I take
a few office supplies here and there?
I deserve them.*

VICTIM VIVIANE has had a rough life, and absolutely none of it is her fault. She is hyper-sensitive and often takes things the wrong way. She blames others for problems that she created and thinks that everyone is out to get her. A chronic drama queen, she makes mountains out of molehills. "I complain a lot solely because I have lots to complain about! The world is against me!"

Draggle Xavier and others are extra careful to not ruffle her antenna or step on her claws. Unfortunately, this means that her work is substandard. And, as you can imagine, she has a suitcase full of excuses about why it's never her fault or responsibility. She won't even take ownership of a small slice of the issue or problem. Rather, she acts like a defenseless child, pities herself, and points her finger at others, including Draggle Xavier ("if only he were a better boss"). Others end up fixing her mistakes or picking up the slack when important work can't be entrusted to her.

Why me?
People are out to get me!

WRIGHT WILBER is always…right, and you're always…wrong. Wright Wilber's specialty is shifting blame rather than dealing with the problem. He focuses on finding out "who" is responsible for a problem, rather than trying to solve the problem. In a moment of apparent openness, he asks for your input, but then he ignores or rapidly discounts it. Wright Wilber expresses strong opinions, making anyone who holds a different opinion immediately wrong. Of course, he assumes that all rational Draggles would agree with his opinion. He frequently adopts a condescending tone and enjoys spouting forth snarky put-downs that make you look stupid. "You say condescending, I say clever."

Watch out! Wright Wilber puts excessive pressure on others to do things his way. If you force his hand, he will exact revenge in some way.

It's my way or the highway.

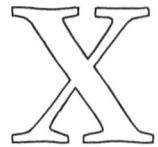

X-CLUSIVE XANE likes to create exclusive cliques. He snubs, ignores and gives the silent treatment to those who aren't worthy of being in his clique. Even during meetings, he doesn't make eye contact or speak with Draggles outside his handpicked clique. He pays little attention to what "the outcasts" have to say and shows little interest in their opinions. X-Clusive Xane is particularly destructive if he's supervising a team: some members are stars, while others are outright excluded.

Only members of his clique are invited to his team social events. The ties between his in-group members are so tight that they help each other out, give each other "inside information" and opportunities, and tell jokes at the expense of outsiders and outcasts who aren't cool enough to be part of his clique. "If you're not one of us, you don't exist!" Outcasts feel like pariah: left out, rejected, and disrespected. X-Clusive Xane talks behind their backs, whispers constantly, and looks at them with derision, if at all. He hosts private, exclusive meetings in his office to spread rumors and gossip about coworkers, closing the door on outcasts who may be walking by.

The ABC's of Uncivil Behavior at Work

*If you're not in my in-group,
you're irrelevant.*

YELLING YOLANDA is a raging bully who wants to have her way every day. She yells, screams, interrupts, and swears. She cuts Draggles off when they're talking and says that she shouldn't have to listen to dribble. She expects you to be at her beck and call. She interrupts your work without hesitation. Yet, her phone messages ("Call me!") are brief and lack the details needed for others to figure out what she wants.

She is argumentative and raises her voice anytime she feels like it; for example, when she doesn't like the tasks assigned to her, when others are doing a poor job (in her eyes), and, especially, if Draggle Xavier challenges her negative behavior. If Yelling Yolanda doesn't get her way, she starts pouting and crying, and she declares herself a helpless victim of her immediate supervisor's oppressive and intimidating treatment. She knows that accusing others of misbehavior takes attention away from her own behavior.

Yelling Yolanda doesn't like to follow the rules or processes that are in place at Zolto Plant. Instead of filling forms and directing them to the Draggle who can address her issues, she contacts that Draggle's boss and complains. Her escalation of her complaints makes other Draggles reluctant to help her.

You exist to serve me ... NOW!

ZUCCHINI ZOË is a close cousin of Mooching Mildred. Zucchini Zoë expects others to clean up after her in the lunchroom. She leaves dirty dishes in the sink, food rotting in the fridge, and tea grounds composting in the sink as well as other things that are likely to plug up the drain. Nor does she clean up microwave splatter. She will empty the coffee pot when pouring herself a cup, but never make a new pot of coffee when the pot is empty. Also, she might snoop in the lunchroom fridge and eat whatever she finds in others' lunch bags.

Her cousins **BARCLAY AND BERTHA BATHROOM** also leave their mark, but in the washroom! Perhaps as a way of saving water or because they don't want to touch the flushing lever, they never flush the toilet. Beware! If you happen to use the toilet stall right after they have been in it, not only will it stink but there will be little shards of toilet paper on the floor, 'liquid' on the floor next to the toilet, brown smears on the toilet seat, and an empty toilet paper holder (because they use a lot of paper, and they bring some home with them). Be careful shaking hands with them because they don't wash their hands after using the toilet. Bertha

Bathroom puts used tampons in or beside the toilet as well as the leftovers from her greasy brown bean lunch. Both Barclay and Bertha Bathroom spend lots of time in the toilet stalls, even when there is a long line-up for them. They wash their lunch dishes in the bathroom sink and leave food residue and puddles of water all around the sink (and sometimes their dishes).

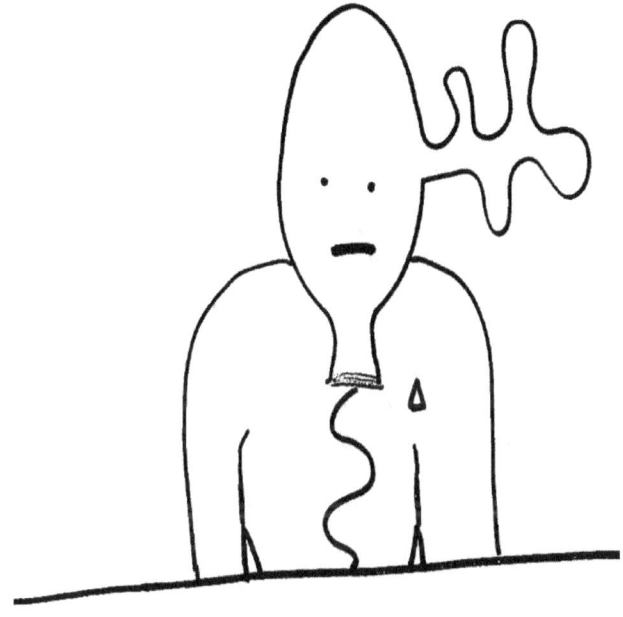

I'm simply too important to clean up after myself.

WOWZERS!

The team of highly perceptive representatives from Planet Wowzer conclude that production at Zolto Plant is suffering due to incivility. Draggle workers are dragging themselves down, feeling stressed, bored or angry, concentrating on themselves, being insensitive to others, and doing everything but focusing on their work.

The ABC's of Uncivil Behavior at Work

Do we look like DUDs or what?

Wowzers can't believe this cast of characters!
All About Me Agnes
Busy Bob & Dabbler Delmar
Credit Hogging Cliff
Downer Dwight
Edith Eater
Fashion Fannie & Unkempt Umberto
Germy George
Harold Hoggler & Harold Haggler
Ill-Mannered & Very Impolite Ida
Judging Judith, Suspicious Susan, & Basil Bully
Karla Kerfuffle
Late & Leaving Larry & Alex AWOL
Mooching Mildred
Needy Ned & Insecure Irma
Opinionated Olga
Personal Space Prunella & Pierre
Quivering Quentin & By the Book Bertram
Rude Randy & Rough Ricky
Socializing Sally
Technology Tommy & Texting Timmy
U Owe Me Uma
Victim Viviane
Wright Wilber
X-Clusive Xane
Yelling Yolanda
Zucchini Zoë & Barclay & Bertha Bathroom

The ABC's of Uncivil Behavior at Work

Those Draggles are the mirror images of Wowzers:
All About Helping Others Agnes
Bob & Delmar Busy but Well Organized & Accountable
Shared Spotlight Cliff
Ray of Sunshine Dwight
Edith Eating with Manners
Properly Groomed Fannie & Umberto
George Gets Well at Home
Harold Happy to Listen & Honor Expectations
Ida Illustratively Super Polite, Civil, and Respectful
Judgement Free & Respectful Judith, Susan, & Basil
Calm and Accepting Karla
Larry & Alex Always in Office and Working
Mildred Hard Worker Who Does Her Share
Ned & Irma Independent & Interdependent in a Team
Olga Open to Other Perspectives
Respectful of Personal Space Prunella & Pierre
Quentin & Bertram Who Take Ownership
Kind Word Randy & Gentle Ricky
Get My Work Done Sally
Respectful of Technology Tommy & Timmy
Uma Self-Directed and Self-Motivated
Viviane Master of her Life
Open to Other Viewpoints Wilber
Inclusive Xane
Courteous Yolanda
Respecting Shared Space Zoë & Barclay & Bertha

AFTER HEARING THE REPORTS OF THEIR REPRESENTATIVES,

Wowzer leaders reflected on their next course of action. It was clear that Draggles were not ready to run the Zolto Plant operation on their own, even with 'dummy-proof' technology. Through much investigation over millennia, Wowzers learned that civility and being a good worker go hand in hand. Incivility = incompetence. Civility is a fundamental requirement of being a good worker. They learned that, if the players in a sandbox don't play well together, the sandbox itself risks being wrecked, metaphorically speaking. What should Wowzers do?

The ABC's of Uncivil Behavior at Work

SHOULD WOWZERS GO AHEAD AND SIMPLY BEAM DOWN and grab the Zolto crystals? Planet Draggle would be easy to invade: Draggles seem to be so focused on themselves and scratching their little sores that they may not notice Wowzers descending upon and visiting their planet's oceans and absorbing their Zolto crystals. But that would involve stealing resources, and Wowzers would never do to Draggles what they wouldn't want to be done to themselves.

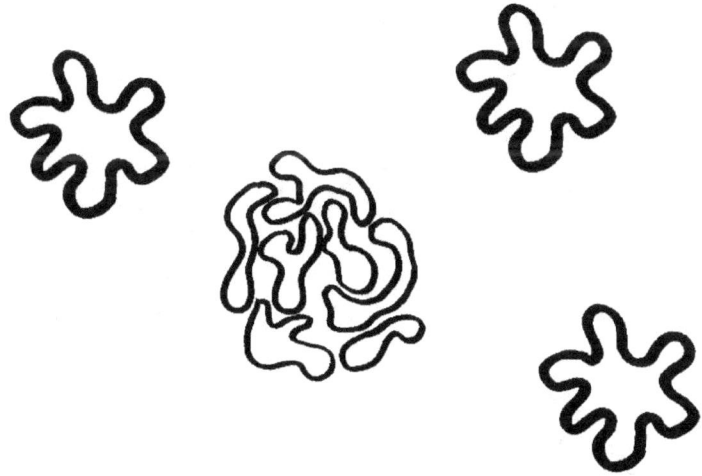

ANOTHER OPTION WOULD BE TO SEND PLANET WOWZIE'S BEST REPRESENTATIVES to Planet Draggle to work alongside Draggles at the Zolto Plant. Through coaching and modeling, they can gradually transform how Draggles interact with each other. By turning Draggle DUDs into WOWs, Draggles would be able to manage the operations smoothly. But would this be possible? And would it take too much time? Is there another option?

What should Wowzers do?

REFLECTION QUESTIONS

1. What alternative endings do you envision for this tale? If you were a Wowzer, what would you do?
2. How might Draggle ways become obstacles in interactions with Wowzers, particularly in managing Zolto Plant?
3. Of the Draggle ways, which do you consider to be the five worst? Why?
4. How would you define civility? Incivility?
5. If you had to order the Draggle ways on a scale from most civil to the least civil, how would your continuum look?
6. What other Draggle ways have you observed that are not included in this tale?
7. How do Draggle ways harm the work environment?
8. What is your usual reaction to Draggle ways?
9. Which five Draggles would you least want to work with on a team? Why?
10. Which Draggles would be most open to changing their ways?
11. What five Draggle ways do you typically see in your workplace?

12. Which five Wowzers would you most want to have on your team? Why? Provide concrete examples of their behaviors.
13. What can coworkers do to discourage Draggle ways and encourage Wowzer behaviors?
14. What will you personally do to discourage Draggle ways and encourage Wowzer behaviors in other coworkers?
15. Which Draggle ways and which Wowzer behaviors represent what you do at work?
16. What will you do differently to:
    a. Eliminate your personal Draggle ways?
    b. Engage in Wowzer behaviors so that you make a positive contribution to the workplace?
17. What can managers do to discourage Draggle ways and encourage Wowzer behaviors?
18. Do you think that even mild versions of Draggle behaviors should be called out because small problems become big problems (the equivalent of 'death by a thousand cuts')? Or… not?
19. Which Draggle ways seem to overlap or fit together well and are likely to form an alliance? Which are more likely to be in conflict?
20. Is it possible for a person to engage in both Draggle AND Wowzer behaviors?
21. What might cause people to engage in Draggle ways?

22. What underlying themes can you see in the Draggle ways?
23. Which of the quotations in the Deep Thoughts section later on in this book appeal to you the most? Why?

ARE YOU A DRAGGLE DUD OR A WOWZER?

These Draggle ways are presented in their extreme caricatured forms as a way of clearly illustrating different types of workplace incivility for the sake of discussion. Almost everyone has displayed one or more of these behaviors to some degree.

The first step to changing your Draggle ways is to figure out what you're doing that isn't working for you or others. You can do this by asking yourself four sets of questions:

1. How do others react to me? Are they happy to see me? Or do they seem to avoid me? Are they simply polite and engaging solely in small talk? Are they itching to get away?
2. What feedback about my behavior have others given me? Sometimes, we fool ourselves. We just don't have any idea that we're screwing up, and we need direct feedback from someone, no matter how much it stings. Asking for and receiving honest feedback from others can be the best thing that ever happened to you, however risky it might feel in the short-term. If you're doing something that is negatively affecting others' perceptions of

you and preventing you from getting the results you want, wouldn't you want to know?

3. What's the impact of what I'm doing? Is it really working for me in the short term or the long term? What sort of relationships am I building with others? Am I growing as a person? Am I truly happy with what I'm doing? Would I be embarrassed to have my behavior described on the front page of the newspaper or Facebook?

4. What does my behavior at work say about my overall approach to life? For example, do I try to give a little (or nothing at all) but get a lot? Do I play the blame and complain game? Do I tend to feel cheated or misunderstood by others? Am I often in a bad mood? Do I wait for others to take the lead and feel frustrated when nothing happens? Am I mainly focused on myself and what I want at the expense of others?

LOOK FOR PATTERNS IN YOUR ANSWERS

Are you behaving more like a Draggle DUD or a Wowzer? Are you generally a civil person? If you're not getting the results you want, if you're feeling crappy about constantly being embroiled in conflict, or if you're not getting much work done, then these are signs that what you're doing isn't working for you. Lots of people don't get to this stage of realization and discomfort. They would rather bury their head in the sand and avoid this business of trying to change Draggle behaviors that feel comfortable but that are just plain ineffective. Congratulate yourself for making the effort to understand your behavior and your results!

CHALLENGE YOUR DRAGGLE DUD WAYS

Being a Draggle is no fun for anyone! Draggle ways bring everyone down and poison the work environment. Draggles seem to lack awareness or consideration for how others see them. They're busy taking but not giving, focusing on what they want at others' expense, and being insensitive to others. In contrast, awesome folks act like Wowzers. People listen to them and want to be around them because they feel respected. If you want to be respected, you've got to be civil. Here are some tips for becoming more civil:

1. **Take responsibility for what you do or don't do.** You're responsible for your behaviors. Whether you realize it or not, you have chosen your behaviors, and you can 'un-choose' them. You're not a puppet on a string. You can exercise self-discipline and self-control. It isn't necessary for you to express every thought, fight every battle, or react to everything that others do or don't do. YOU choose. You retain agency and the freedom to make your own choices and take responsibility for the results of your choices.

2. **Keep in mind that no one can hurt your feelings.** Negative feelings are signals that what you're doing or thinking isn't helping you meet your needs. Restructure (change) how you think about things, and you'll change how you feel. Two people can be in the same situation and interpret it differently. It's our interpretations of things that often get us into trouble, especially when we think that someone has intentionally tried to hurt us. Ask yourself how you can interpret a situation differently.

3. **Give people the benefit of the doubt.** Ask them what's going on. Don't automatically assume that someone's out to get you. They may have made a mistake unintentionally. You haven't walked a mile in their shoes. They may be going through a hard time personally or professionally, so their behavior may be out of whack. And, there may be a policy or other situational factors influencing their behavior. Making assumptions about why other people do things gets us into trouble. Besides, we're all human. No one's perfect. Holding on to resentments and anger hurts you more than other people.

4. **Communicate directly with the person involved.** Don't talk with everyone about the problem you're having with Person X; this makes you part of the problem, not the solution. Instead, choose the right moment, and talk directly with Person X. Calmly.

   Share your observations, and then your interpretations. Try to agree on the facts, and be open to other interpretations. Take responsibility whenever you can. Don't cut others off or walk away in mid-sentence. Listen. Wait till they have finished saying what they have to say. Don't get angry, don't accuse, don't yell, don't be hostile, don't call people names, don't pout, don't threaten, don't be rude, don't guilt-trip, don't roll your eyes, don't point your finger, don't order, and don't push. That's not how you make friends and influence people. And, none of these behaviors are effective, at least in the long run. Someone might agree to your demands in the short term just to get you off their back but you lose their respect, and you lose the game in the long run. It's hard to repair a relationship that you've broken through bad behavior.

5. **Be polite and respectful.** Courtesy doesn't take extra time or effort, and it allows others to see you as a reasonable person who is in control of yourself. Saying please, thank you, sorry, excuse me and other expressions of politeness are simple ways to show that you respect others. Also, cleaning up after yourself is basic politeness. And don't disturb others or get into their personal space. If you want others to respect you, you have to show them respect first.

6. **Get rid of your sense of entitlement.** It just gets in your way and makes people think that you haven't grown up yet. You are not the Center of the Universe. Don't think that everything has to be handed to you on a silver plate, or that everything has to go your way. Others do not exist to serve you. Mature adults realize that they have rights AND responsibilities as do those around them. If your focus is on your rights and what's due to you, you'll likely trample on the rights of others because you'll see people as being in your way. You can't always get what you want, but you can try to get some of your needs met while respecting the rights of others to do the same.

7. **Put things in perspective.** Really now, how important is that …? Is it going to make a huge difference in your life? When you look back 10 or 20 years from now, what do you think will be most important to you? Are you willing to yell and scream while pushing for what you want, but damage the relationship in the process? Sometimes, we get stuck in the rut of the moment, we ruminate, and we just can't see our way out of the mess we create for ourselves. But, things get better, and, in the long run, minor irritations are meaningless. Don't waste your time scratching little sores. Focus on what is really important.

8. **Be professional.** Ask yourself, "What would a professional do in this situation?" No Draggle behaviors, however justified in your mind, are what we see successful professionals doing. If you want to be a professional (and be viewed as a professional), start now, by acting in a mature, calm, considerate and reasonable manner. Remember: incivility is just another form of incompetence.

9. **Be positive and agreeable.** If you have the choice between being positive and being negative (and, by the way, we all have this choice in every circumstance), why not be positive? Being negative hurts you, your reputation, your results, your relationships, and, yes, your body. It brings you down physically, mentally, socially, and spiritually. You probably don't realize how horrible you look to others when you're being a jerk. When you're behaving like a jerk to someone, they just want to be a jerk right back to you. Emotions are contagious and have a ripple effect on those around you. So, be aware of what you're projecting and radiating to others. Are you sapping them of energy, or are you helping others feel more energized?

10. **Use humor**, when appropriate, to deal with potentially embarrassing or difficult situations. This demonstrates your humanity, softens the tone of exchanges, and helps people save face. More importantly, learn to laugh at yourself, admit your errors, and be generous with others.

11. **Practice the Golden Rule "Do unto others as you would have them do unto you" and the Platinum Rule, "Treat others the way they want to be treated."** Civility means respecting others and regarding every person as being worthy of consideration, whether we like or agree with them. If everyone took responsibility for behaving in a civil manner, then we would create a civil society. Are you strengthening the goodwill that exists in this world, or are you a weak link?

12. **Focus on the positive things that others contribute, and show gratitude whenever possible.** As leadership expert Ken Blanchard suggests, "Catch people doing something right," and let them know that you appreciate them. It shows that you're a team player who works well with others rather than competing with them, stealing their ideas, or focusing on their errors. Yes, even people in positions of authority such as your manager need to feel that they are appreciated. We are all people who need people. When you disrespect or dismiss someone, you're telling them that they are of little worth to you. These undermining behaviors can destroy someone's sense of self-worth.

13. **Try to adopt a spirit of openness at all times.** Life is an amazing cornucopia of experiences and opportunities. There are different ways to solve problems, work, learn, and experience the world. You have found a "way of being" in this world that is comfortable for you, but others also have their own perspectives. Trying to be flexible, stepping out of your comfort zone, and being open to other ways of being and doing things will help you grow as a person. It will also help you become more creative when you're faced with new situations.

14. **Be a source of learning and light for others.** Try to be a "vessel of learning" and help others learn things through you. Being a good co-worker means not only being a good example for others but also taking the initiative to help those who may be having trouble.

15. **Be realistic and get organized.** Don't overload yourself with commitments. Figure out how to manage your time, your mood and yourself well, and do it. This is a basic skill for success at work, school, and home. Try to learn this lesson as early in life as possible. Procrastination is a dead end, a sure way to fail. You might be able to procrastinate and get by in the short term, but getting by isn't the same as succeeding. That rush that you get that spurs you to finish a report at the last minute is interpreted by your body as stress, and stress can do nasty things to your body (hypertension, fatigue, sleep disturbances, anxiety, digestion problems, etc.).

16. **Realize that learning at work is an investment that you make in yourself.** You're only hurting yourself by not learning how to do your job well or by minimizing how much time and effort you put into your work. Make your work your priority while you're at work, and you'll like the results. You'll be proud of yourself!

17. **Clean up after yourself. Don't steal other people's stuff. Share. Smile. Co-operate.**

CHALLENGE OTHERS' INCIVILITY

Ah, this is a sticky topic. Although you may be tempted to adopt uncivil behaviors as a way of eradicating them in others, this tit-for-tat approach only generates a negative downward spiral of incivility. So, **retaliation and confrontation are not the answer**. As Yoda would say, "challenge incivility, you must." **Keeping quiet about uncivil behaviors says that you condone them.** As a result, they may continue or even escalate. **And trying to avoid uncivil folks may be difficult if you have to work with them on a day-to-day basis.** How you approach others can be the difference between hostile reactions and changed behaviors.

More often than not, folks who engage in uncivil behaviors are not aware that what they're doing is disrespectful or that it's having a negative impact on others. So, a good first step is to organize a **"Civility Awareness Session"** that allows you to (a) get everyone on the same page regarding what civility is and isn't; (b) clarify expectations, and (c) develop an agreement regarding norms for civil behavior going forward. In preparing for this session, all participants should read a copy of this book and answer the reflection questions that are presented. The Civility Awareness Session can consist of an open discussion of the answers to the questions and the development of civility "rules" or expectations that all agree to follow. If you're not in a position to organize this session, you can recommend it to your manager or someone in Human Resources.

As an individual, you can **challenge uncivil behaviors in an assertive, respectful, and non-confrontational manner**, ideally, as soon as they occur. Express your needs directly, and clarify the effects of others' behavior on you. Try to use key phrases such as the following: "The effects of this behavior on me are…, I feel…, I prefer…, etc." This will prevent you from framing your concerns using "you," which comes across as an attack on another person. This technique is similar to the **DESC technique** developed by assertiveness specialists Sharon Bower and Gordon Bower. DESC involves communicating assertively by **d**escribing, **e**xpressing, **s**pecifying, and targeting the **c**onsequences. First, **describe** the situation by sticking to the facts without making value judgments. Second, **express** your reactions to the situation (describe your thoughts and emotions) using "I" statements. Third, be **specific** about your expectations and needs; explain your desired outcome. Finally, express the **consequences** of reaching or not reaching a solution. As incivility expert Christine Porath suggests in her *Harvard Business Review* article, you need to prepare what you're going to say, perhaps rehearsing it with another person, pay attention to your nonverbal signals, and focus on the person's behavior and its effects (not the person).

Wait! Before giving others feedback about their behavior, you may wish to heed Christine Porath's advice. She suggests that you **avoid talking with others if your answer to the following questions is "no"**: "(1) Do I feel safe talking with this person? (2) Was the behavior intentional? (3) Was it the only instance of such behavior by him or her?" In other words, if you feel unsafe or if the behavior was accidental or unconscious and a rare occurrence, then don't talk to this person about it. Rather, she suggests that you, "Concentrate on your own effectiveness and, in future encounters, follow the acronym BIFF: Be *brief, informative, friendly,* and *firm*."

If approaching the individual is too risky, and the person is likely to react poorly, then you may find it useful to **talk to your manager or someone in HR** about the behavior. Hopefully, they have the courage to stamp out the toxic behavior. Unfortunately and for whatever reason, your manager's or HR's hands may be tied, and, as a result, their solutions have no impact on the problem. Why? Well, sometimes, there isn't a desire to deal with the incivility because the uncivil people are politically connected, they bring in lots of business or money into the organization, or something else. As a result, incivility is tolerated, accepted, and, indeed, celebrated rather than managed and "disciplined."

In these cases, the solution resides with you and how you take care of yourself when faced with toxic behavior. **Aside from modeling civil behavior, you need to buffer yourself from others' incivility.** Don't take others' incivility personally and brood over it. Rather, you should focus on making a positive contribution to the workplace and actively managing the stress associated with others' incivility (by journaling, seeking support, managing your energy, or changing how you think and feel about the behaviors). Being exposed to incivility on an ongoing basis can erode your personal health – emotionally, physically, and spiritually. Ultimately, you have a decision point ahead of you: do you *fit* in an organization that seems to turn a blind eye to incivility? Is there a kinder, gentler, more "adult" workplace beckoning?

DEEP THOUGHTS

"Whoever one is, and wherever one is, one is always in the wrong if one is rude." — Maurice Baring

"Remember there's no such thing as a small act of kindness. Every act creates a ripple with no logical end." — Scott Adams

"There is no beautifier of complexion, or form, or behavior, like the wish to scatter joy and not pain around us." — Ralph Waldo Emerson

"Remember not only to say the right thing in the right place but far more difficult still, to leave unsaid the wrong thing at the tempting moment." — Benjamin Franklin

"This is the first test of a gentleman: his respect for those who can be of no possible value to him." — William Lyon Phelps

"Whenever there is a human being, there is an opportunity for a kindness." — Lucious Annaeus, *Seneca*

"Life is what our relationships make it....Good relationships make our lives good; bad relationships make our lives bad....To learn how to be happy, we must learn how to live well with others, and civility is a key to that." —P.M. Forni, *Choosing Civility*

"Life is relational. Whether we like it or not, we are wax upon which others leave their mark. When someone sees us as a thing to use or abuse, that becomes part of who we are in our own eyes as well (self-esteem notwithstanding), When we are on the receiving end of an act of kindness, we feel validated. We translate that act into a very simple, very powerful unspoken message to ourselves: I am not alone, I have value and my life has meaning." —P.M. Forni, *Choosing Civility*

"When the healthy pursuit of self-interest and self-realization turns into self-absorption, other people can lose their intrinsic value in our eyes and become mere means to the fulfillment of our needs and desires."
— P.M. Forni, *The Civility Solution*

"When you know you can do something, and you feel good about yourself, you do not have to devalue others." — John Patrick Hickey, *Oops! Did I Really Post That*

"Wisdom tells us that the best time for silence is when we are mad or upset." — John Patrick Hickey, *Oops! Did I Really Post That*

"You don't have to prove confidence; when you have it, it'll show. Real confidence is quiet, tactful, civil, and humble." — Rosalinda Oropez Randall, *Don't Burp in the Boardroom: Your Guide to Handling Uncommonly Common Workplace Dilemmas*

"A talent for forgetting is necessary to maintain civility." —Matthew De Abaitua, *If Then*

"When once the forms of civility are violated, there remains little hope of a return to kindness or decency." — Samuel Johnson

"The happiness of your life depends upon the quality of your thoughts." — Marcus Aurelius

"Emotional competence implies we have a choice as to how we express our feelings." — Dan Goleman

"We have a choice about how we behave, and that means we have the choice to opt for civility and grace." — Dwight Currie

"Respecting the 'No' of another is one of the most elementary and significant rules of respect." — P.M. Forni

"What is civility if not a constant awareness that no human encounter is without consequence?" — P.M. Forni

"Manners are based on an ideal of empathy, of imagining the impact of one's own actions on others. They involve doing something for the sake of other people that is not obligatory and attracts no reward." — Lynne Truss, *Talk to the Hand*

"The interesting thing is that, cut free from any sense of community, we are miserable and lonely as well as rude. This is an age of social autism, in which people just can't see the value of imagining their impact on others, and in which responsibility is always conveniently laid at other people's doors." — Lynne Truss, *Talk to the Hand*

"Civility costs nothing, and buys everything." — Mary Wortley Montagu

SUGGESTED READING

Sharon Anthony Bower & Gordon Bower (2004). *Asserting Yourself - Updated Edition: A Practical Guide for Positive Change*

P.M. Forni (2003). *Choosing Civility: The Twenty-five Rules of Considerate Conduct*

P.M. Forni (2009). *The Civility Solution: What to do When People are Rude*

John Patrick Hickey (2015). *Oops! Did I Really Post That: Online Etiquette in the New Digital Age*

M. Scott Peck (1997). *A World Waiting to be Born: Search for Civility*

Christine Porath (2016). An antidote to incivility. *Harvard Business Review*

Rosalinda Oropez Randall (2014). *Don't Burp in the Boardroom: Your Guide to Handling Uncommonly Common Workplace Dilemmas*

Lynne Truss (2005). *Talk to the Hand: The Utter Bloody Rudeness of the World Today or Six Good Reasons to Stay Home and Bolt the Door*

www.ingramcontent.com/pod-product-compliance
Lightning Source LLC
Chambersburg PA
CBHW052334220526
45472CB00001B/415